Everything You Need To Know

WHEN A
PARENT DIES

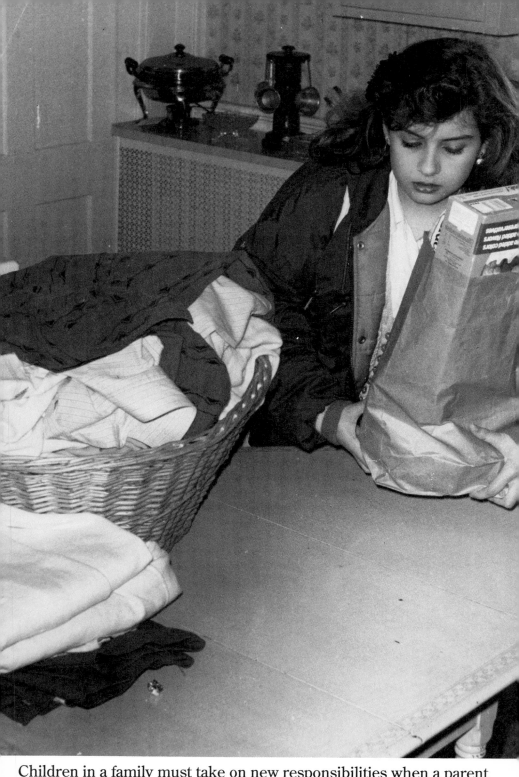

Children in a family must take on new responsibilities when a parent dies.

• THE NEED TO KNOW LIBRARY •

Everything You Need To Know
WHEN A
PARENT DIES

Fred Bratman

THE ROSEN PUBLISHING GROUP, INC.
NEW YORK

For Jack's Memory

Published in 1992, 1995, 1998 by The Rosen Publishing Group, Inc.
29 East 21st Street, New York, NY 10010

Revised Edition 1998

Library of Congress Cataloging-in-Publication Data

Bratman, Fred
    Everything you need to know when a parent dies/
    (The Need to know library)
    Includes bibliographical references and index.
    Summary: A guide to coping with the stresses and emotions arising after the death of a parent.
    ISBN 0-8239-2870-5
    1. Bereavement in children—Juvenile literature. 2. Parents—death—Psychological aspects—Juvenile literature. 3. Children and death—Juvenile literature. 4. Grief in children—Juvenile literature. [1. Death. 2. Parent and child.] United States—Juvenile literature. I. Title. II. Series.
    BF723.G75873 1992
    155.9'37—dc20
                                               90-27488
                                                   CIP
                                                       AC

Manufactured in the United States of America

Contents

Introduction

Death can be a scary subject. Many people don't like to talk about it. They don't want to make themselves or others sad. Talking about death makes people realize they, too, will grow old and die one day.

You may already have experienced the death of someone you care about—a grandparent, a neighbor, or a beloved pet. After this death, you probably felt sad and upset. Eventually your feelings got easier to handle, and you probably began to remember the good times you had with this loved one. In time, sadness lessened and more peaceful feelings took its place.

However, the death of a parent is especially traumatic. A parent takes care of you, listens to your worries, lends a shoulder to cry on, and cheers your accomplishments. You have a special relationship with your parent. A parent's death affects you differently than that of others you may have lost. The feelings are deeper and stronger and may seem overwhelming.

One powerful emotion that you experience when a parent dies is called grief. Grief is very intense emotional suffering that a traumatic event causes. Grief doesn't feel good—it hurts—but it is necessary. A person needs to grieve to be able to accept someone's death and to say good-bye to that person.

Grief can last a long time. But eventually it lessens and finally disappears. The sadness becomes bearable and easier to talk about. After your grief eases, you will once again remember the happy times you shared with your parent. You may never completely stop longing for your parent, but you will be able to go on with your life.

If one of your parents has died, you may wonder, Who will be there for me? Your life may change drastically after a parent's death. You may have to live with your other parent or a relative. That may mean moving to a new city or school. You may have to live in a foster home. You may have to get a part-time job to help out with expenses or take on more chores at home. But whatever happens, you will be cared for. This book will explain how.

You will also read stories about other teenagers whose parents have died. You will see that they, too, had painful and frightening feelings after their parent died. They know what you're going through. These teens will share the ways they eased their pain.

Most important, this book will help you understand why you should talk about your feelings. Stuffing your feelings deep down won't make them go away. When you don't express your feelings, then the emotions seem overwhelming and too hard to handle. When you talk to someone else, you help yourself to conquer your painful and uncomfortable feelings. Remember, you don't have to bear your grief alone. There are others who care about you and want to help you deal with your parent's death.

The death of a parent can make it hard for children to concentrate or think of anything else.

Chapter 1

The Loss of a Parent

The death of a parent is one of the most difficult things you can live through. As an adult, losing a parent is a sad experience. It is often even worse for a child or teenager. The death of a parent can cause serious and permanent changes in a child's or teenager's life.

Earlier, we described what grief is. Now you need to know about the stages of grief. Some people go through all of them, but others do not. There is no fixed pattern of grieving, since everyone grieves in his or her own way. There is also no set time period to reach acceptance of a parent's death. And in between all of these stages is immense sorrow and sadness.

When a parent dies, your initial reaction may be shock and confusion.

"I never imagined my dad would have a heart attack. After all, he was pretty young. He seemed healthy. I just can't believe it.

"Why did this have to happen? It doesn't make sense. What's Mom going to do? What am I going to do?"

Right now, fifteen-year-old Sam is feeling numb with shock because of his father's death. No one in Sam's family, including his dad, knew his father was at risk for a heart attack. No one was prepared for his death, least of all Sam. Sam's numbness will lessen in time as his shock wears off.

Eventually Sam will feel a wave of sorrow and sadness. It may hit him powerfully all at once, or it may gradually build in strength. But Sam is beginning his journey through the grieving process. He's also talking about his feelings with his mother. In turn, his mother is talking about her future plans with Sam. That way, he doesn't feel frightened by not knowing what will happen to the family. Sam is taking the first steps in dealing with his grief.

Ignoring the Painful Truth

Some people go into denial after the death of a loved one. Denial is ignoring or suppressing one's true feelings and refusing to admit the reality of the situation. People may not want to recognize that their loved one is dead. It is too painful for them to admit that they won't ever see their parent again.

People use denial to escape from a painful event. You can use your imagination to pretend something has not really happened. A parent's death can make you feel as if you want to run away. In most cases you cannot really run somewhere else—and doing so wouldn't help anyway—so you escape inside yourself.

If you think you may be in denial, be patient with yourself. Eventually you will have to admit the truth and accept your parent's death. Try not to get frustrated wondering when your denial will end. Give yourself the time you need. It's not easy to let go of the special relationship you had with your parent.

Angry Feelings

Other people become angry when faced with death. For example, although you may know your parent did not intend to get sick, you may be angry that he or she left you. You may be furious that your parent wasn't able to prevent his or her death from happening. It's okay to be angry. Don't feel guilty about it. Feelings aren't right or wrong, they just are.

Also, don't get upset with your brother or sister if he or she is angry at your parent for dying. Let your sibling express his or her feelings. Showing your emotions is part of the grieving process.

Other times, you may be angry simply at the fact that your parent has died. You may not know whom to blame. But blaming someone won't make your feelings go away. Examine what is underneath your anger. Often it's fear or sadness. Many people turn their hurt into anger. But working your way through denial and anger will put you more quickly on the path to accepting your parent's death. You'll learn more about acceptance in Chapter 6.

Big and Little Changes

The weeks and months following a parent's death are very difficult. Your home may not feel the same without your mom or dad. And, you're right, things aren't the same. But change is a part of life. Whether the change is good or bad, it is almost always stressful because you have to adapt to a new situation. Dealing with change takes time.

Some kids have to move to a different apartment or house. For many families, the loss of a parent also means the loss of income. Your living parent may not be able to afford the existing mortgage or rent.

A new home may even be in another city or state. This change may be particularly stressful because you will have to say good-bye to your old friends and neighbors. You'll have to make new friends and get used to a new place. It takes time to adjust and fit in.

Sometimes children or teens may be sent to a relative's home to live. A parent may need time alone to cope with his or her grief. He or she may also need time alone to get details, such as living arrangements and financial affairs, in order. Your parent may not be able to give you the care and attention you need and deserve while he or she is trying to work things out. Another relative may be in a better position to give you support, with both day-to-day living and emotions.

Other kids are sent to live permanently with relatives or foster parents. A foster parent offers to provide a home for and care for children who are not relatives. Moving into a foster home means adjusting

Things can change dramatically when a family loses a parent. Sometimes it is necessary for the remaining family to sell their house or move to another neighborhood.

to a new family. You have to adapt to your relatives or foster parents, their household, and their rules. You may also have to attend a new school, depending on where your relatives or foster family live.

It's okay to feel scared if you have to move. You may not feel at home right away, but you may be able to ease your feelings by honestly communicating with your relatives or foster parents. They will become your caregivers. They will provide you with not only food and clothing but nurturing, guidance, and discipline. Being honest about your needs and your feelings is one way to help ensure that your move will go smoothly.

Other kids will be able to stay in their homes after their parent dies. However, they may have to take on more responsibilities at home. They may have to baby-sit their younger siblings or cook dinner while their parent works. Some teenagers will need to get a part-time job to help out with expenses. When a parent dies, one less person is available to run a household and a family. Everyone has to pitch in and help.

Helping out with chores or finances can enable you to feel important to your family. This may ease the pain of grieving. But don't try to take over the role of a parent completely. That's too much of a responsibility to take on as a teenager. You still need to be able to live your life.

Chapter 2

A Flood of Emotions

Tracy's Diary

My mother died when I was 14. I had to take on all kinds of new responsibilities, and I was somehow expected to be a mother to my little brother and sister. I did the cooking, the cleaning, the grocery shopping, the laundry, the baby-sitting . . . it just got to be way too much to handle. I fell behind on my schoolwork and had no time for my friends. I was very unhappy, but I couldn't ignore my responsibilities. I felt that I had to grow up fast even though I was still just a kid. Nobody should try to be a mother at 14.

What happened to Tracy happens to a lot of teens when one or both of their parents die. They are already coping with pain and grief, but they also feel a lot of new stress and pressure to fulfill the role of the dead parent. But a teenager cannot fulfill an adult role as a grown-up mother or father can. A teenager cannot be expected to become an adult overnight. Becoming an adult is a slow and gradual process that cannot be rushed.

Tracy's father wanted her to take care of her brother and sister the way her mother did. He was not considering Tracy's feelings, but she did not want to let her father down. So she did her best to be a mother.

Other important areas of Tracy's life began to suffer. At 14, she should have been focusing her energy on doing well in school and making friends. Instead she cooked, cleaned, and took care of her siblings with her free time. This made it more difficult for her to overcome the loss of her mother. Not only was she dealing with her grief, but she was also starting to feel depressed because of her slipping grades. She felt like a failure.

Finally, Tracy's principal called her father, who was very angry when he was told that Tracy was doing poorly in school. Because of his own suffering, he could not understand that his actions were part of the reason Tracy had problems with her studies.

When she came home from school that day, her father was waiting for her. "What's wrong?" Tracy asked when she saw the angry look on his face.

"What's wrong? You're failing four classes, that's what's wrong!" he shouted.

Friends are an important source of comfort and security during times of great sadness.

Even though a parent is gone, his or her memory will stay with you for the rest of your life.

"Dad, since Mom died, I've had a lot to do. I haven't had time to study."

This only made her father angrier. "How dare you blame your mother's death for your own laziness!" he snapped at her.

"Laziness!" Tracy shouted. "I work harder than any 14-year-old in the world!"

Her father started to cry. "My wife just died. I don't need this from you. I need your help."

Tracy ran to her room in tears and slammed the door. She did not want to fight with her father or upset him, but she was angry. Too much was being asked of her, and it was too soon.

Tracy needs to tell her father how scared and angry she feels. They need to discuss their feelings together. Tracy should explain to her father that she is hurting and that she misses her mother too. This is the first and most important step on the way to coping with death. She needs to tell him that she is not ready to be an adult or take on the responsibilities of an adult. She can also let her father know that she wants to help him in any way that she can, but she also needs time for herself to study, do homework, and spend time with her friends.

It is natural to feel a flood of emotions when your parent dies. Experiencing so many painful feelings at one time can be confusing. You may feel that the only way to go on is to believe that your parent is still alive. You know it's not true, but you act as if it were. This sort of denial is called a *defense*. It is a way of holding back the flood of emotions that you feel.

Caring for a parent who is terminally ill takes great courage and compassion.

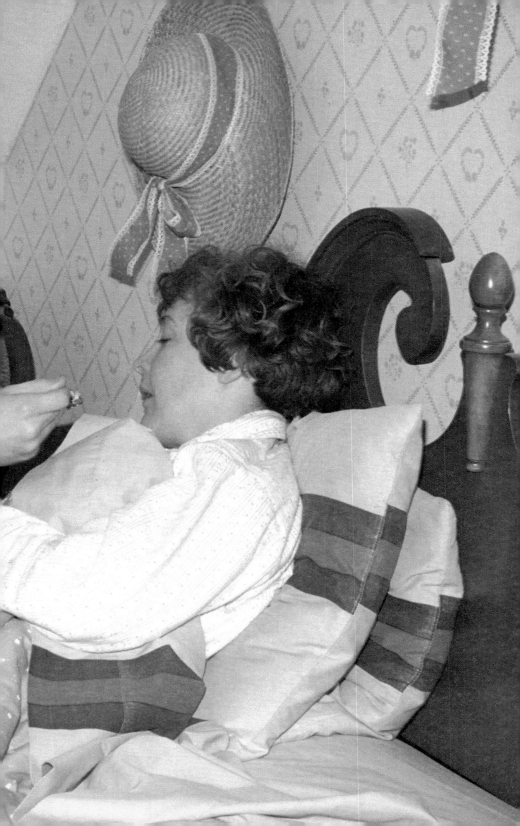

Blaming Yourself

Unfortunately, it's a fact of life: People die, and sometimes they die at a young age. Losing a parent is painful and difficult. This is true whether your parent has died after a long illness or has died suddenly as the result of a car accident.

It's important to realize that the death is not your fault. Nothing you did or could have done would have prevented it. It was out of your control.

Allyson and her mother got into an argument one night after dinner. Allyson's mother planned to go out to meet some friends. But Allyson knew that her mother had been drinking and shouldn't be driving.

Her mother, though, was in a bad mood. When Allyson suggested that someone come to pick her up, she yelled that she didn't need anyone, least of all a sixteen-year-old, telling her what to do.

"Mom, you shouldn't drink and drive," Allyson said. "Please don't go. Give me the keys."

"I'm perfectly capable of driving. I've only had a couple of drinks," her mother said. "And I certainly don't need you taking care of me."

"Come on, Mom. You could get hurt or, even worse, hurt someone else. Give me the keys. I mean it," Allyson responded. She tried to grab the car keys, but her mother pushed her away and headed out the door.

Allyson sighed, disgusted. She had been through this before with her mother. It never seemed to end. Her mother's drinking had gotten worse over the years.

The family order often changes after the death of a parent. In many cases, older siblings must assume the role of caretaker for younger family members.

Allyson knew that one day something bad was going to happen.

Around midnight, Allyson's father woke her up. Right away she knew that something was terribly wrong. He told her that her mother had been in an accident. She had been drunk and speeding and had lost control of her car. She didn't survive.

"Dad, I should have stopped her," Allyson cried. "I should have done more. Then she wouldn't be dead. It's all my fault."

Allyson's father knew that Allyson wasn't to blame for her mother's death. Her mother chose to drink and drive. Allyson was not responsible for her actions. She is responsible only for herself. Allyson was blaming herself for something that was beyond her control.

Allyson's father helped her see that she wasn't responsible for her mother's behavior. Sometimes when you feel guilty, you need someone else to help you see the truth.

After a parent's death, some people turn their guilt into anger. They express their anger by getting into fights, hurting people, or damaging property. The best way to deal with this anger is to talk to someone.

Talking about your feelings—whether they are guilt, anger, sadness, or others—is the only way to overcome them. If you don't share them with someone, the feelings will return again and again. Only by facing them can you conquer them.

Chapter 3

Grieving from a Distance

These days, living with one parent is very common. Many, many kids live with either their mom or dad. Some kids live with their grandparents or other relatives. That doesn't have to change the love you feel for the parent who doesn't live with you.

Anne's parents were divorced. Her father now lived in another part of town. She saw her father on weekends and lived with him during the summer school break. Her father had remarried. He had a son and a daughter with his new wife. Anne enjoyed her visits with her father. But she didn't like her father's new wife. Anne said her father's wife was mean to her.

One day Anne got home from her after-school job at the supermarket as the phone rang. Her father's wife was very upset. Anne's father had been shot. "The funeral is Wednesday at 9 a.m. Have your mother drive you over to the church by 8:30."

Anne started to cry. She couldn't believe what she had heard. She felt like she'd been given an electric shock. Her mother asked, "What's wrong?"

"Dad is dead. He was killed in a robbery." "I won't miss your father," her mother said. "He left me in the middle of the night without a dime." Anne stood there crying.

Anne's mother was not thinking about Anne's feelings. She was only thinking about the pain Anne's father had caused her. What Anne needed was support from her mother. She needed someone to share her grief with. She needed someone who would make her feel safe. Her mother was not able to give this to Anne. She was still angry at Anne's father, even though they were divorced 10 years ago.

For Anne, her father was still her father. She still loved him. Anne's mother doesn't understand Anne's feelings. This happens often in families where parents are divorced. Anne's father was kind to her. He didn't stop being her father when he moved out. Things were different for her mother. He did stop being her husband.

At the funeral, her father's wife spoke only a few words to Anne. There were many people there who she had never seen before. She felt like an outsider.

It can be difficult to grieve the loss of a parent in a family where the divorce or separation has already caused anger and pain.

Anne sat next to an uncle who had always been warm to her. They talked about how sad they were about her father's death. They told stories about the good times they had together. Anne felt less alone. She felt comfortable crying in front of her uncle. A few days later her uncle called to see how she was doing. They spoke for nearly an hour. They laughed and cried and remembered more stories about her father.

When You Are Far Away

Anne was lucky. She saw her father often after her parents divorced. That isn't always possible. Sometimes a parent leaves home and moves to a new city hundreds of miles away. This is hard on kids. They don't get to see that parent often. Sometimes they get together only once or twice a year. They only see each other at holidays, or during the summer. Sometimes they cannot visit at all.

Even a child who didn't see his parent often feels angry and sad when that parent dies. He or she probably thought that someday they would spend time together. The child is angry because that dream is taken away.

What happens to kids whose parents are divorced when the parent they are living with dies? Their living parent may live hundreds of miles away in another state. He or she may have a new family.

There is no single answer.

Counselors can help people sort out feelings of grief, confusion, and loneliness.

Some parents eagerly want their children to live with them and their new families. But many times this is not possible.

In some cases, a state or local child care agency will get involved. You will be interviewed by a case worker. You may appear in front of judge in family court. You are not there because you have done anything wrong. It's the judge's job to make sure that your new home is the best one for you.

Sometimes the best place to send you is to your grandparents or other close relatives. When this is not possible, you may be placed with foster parents.

Daniel's mother moved more than 2,000 miles away when she divorced. Daniel spoke to his

Ordinary things around the house will remind the family of the parent it has lost.

mother on the telephone. But sometimes weeks would pass between calls. Daniel wouldn't have much to say to his mom. Daniel used to spend two weeks with his mother each summer. But he skipped his visit this year. He didn't feel comfortable around his mother anymore. The last time they got together they argued a lot. Daniel wasn't sure what he wanted to do after he finished high school.

One night when Daniel was sitting around watching television, the phone rang. It was one of his mother's friends. He told Daniel that he had bad news for him. His mother was dead.

Living apart from a parent doesn't make death less painful for kids. Even though Daniel was not getting along with his mother, he could still remember the good times they had together. The importance of a relationship is not based on whether your parent lives with you. There is more to it than that. The way you feel about the person is what's important. If what you remember is good, then you will probably be very sad.

When a child loses a parent who lives far away, he or she grieves just like other kids. Except it's harder. Your friends may not understand why you are so upset. Perhaps they never met your mom or dad. They don't know how strong your feelings are. Your grief is as painful as it would be if the parent lived with you. You have a right to feel sadness, no matter how far away your parent lived.

Visiting a hospital can be a scary and uncomfortable experience. It requires courage to fulfill the responsibility you may have to a loved one.

Chapter 4

In the Hospital

Jason knew his mother was sick. But he didn't know she was seriously ill. She had been sick for nearly six months. She had been seeing several different doctors. At dinner one night his mom told Jason that she had to go to the hospital. She needed an operation. Jason was scared.

"I'm not going to treat you like a baby," she told him. "I'll tell you what I know. The doctors tell me that I have cancer." Jason couldn't believe his ears. His mother looked healthy to him. "I'll be in the hospital at least a week, maybe longer," she said. "I'll need you to help out with your sister while I'm away from home."

Jason didn't know what to say. He opened his mouth but no words came out. The next day Jason's mother went to the hospital. After school, Jason went to visit her. She was sitting up in bed, but she looked weak. A tube was connected to her arm. She had trouble speaking.

Jason felt like he was in a bad dream. "If only I could wake up," he thought. Then the sadness would go away. But this wasn't a dream.

The nurses and doctors came into the room. Jason asked a doctor what was wrong with his mother. The doctor told Jason that his mother was sick. He said he was going to do all he could to make her well again.

"There's so much I want to say," Jason said to a friend. "But I don't know where to start, I don't want to say anything stupid."

Jason didn't know what to say to his mother. He had only known her as a strong woman. He didn't understand how she could have become weak so quickly.

If your parent is sick in a hospital, figuring out what to say is often hard. You may even feel that the person in the bed is different from your parent. Remember that he or she is the same person. The only difference is that he or she is sick.

Try to talk the way you would if your parent wasn't in a hospital. If you usually talked about your school work, bring in some school work to show your mom or dad. If you both always like to

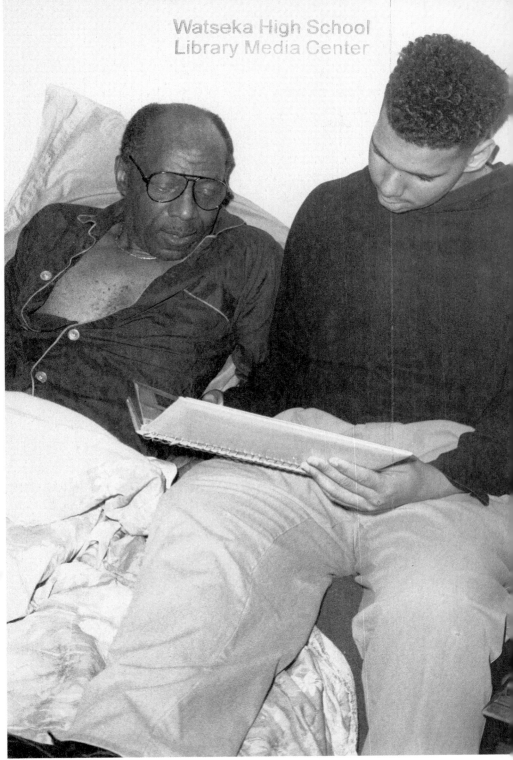

The most comforting thing for a sick person is the company of others.

talk about sports, talk about the latest games and team standings.

Sometimes other adults will tell you what to say in the hospital. They'll say, "Smile, don't let her see you upset. Don't upset her." These adults mean well. But faking it could easily make matters worse. Be honest. Tell your parent how you feel. Parents want to know that they still matter to you. Tell your parent that you really need him or her. But try not to make your parent worry about you. Try to be bright and cheerful.

When your parent is in the hospital, he or she will worry about how life is at home. Your parent will want to know who is cooking for you. He or she will ask about who's helping you with your algebra homework. If you are the oldest child at home, much of the work will fall to you. You may resent the added chores. You may think that school work is enough to keep you busy. But illness in a family means that everyone has to help.

Jason's mother asked him to pick up his younger sister after school every day and bring her to a neighbor. He was also responsible now for buying groceries. And he had to do the laundry for the family. The added work meant that he had to quit the track team. This made Jason angry. He thought he had a chance to make the state championships. He wanted to be helpful at home. But he also wanted to do some things for himself.

All the added work had a bad effect on Jason. He easily became angry at his younger sister. She was giving him a lot of trouble. Jason had to understand something important. His sister was also scared by what was happening to their mother.

At school, Jason's grades were slipping. Grades often drop when a student's parent is very ill. Jason told his teacher that his mother was in the hospital. He explained that he had to help around the house. "I didn't have time to do my homework," Jason said. The teacher said that the work had to be done. But she said that Jason could turn it in to her after his mother got home from the hospital.

Jason's mother returned home after the operation. But over the next year she often had to go for treatment of her cancer. She became weaker. Jason had to continue to do more work at home. He was often tired. He was angry at his mother's illness. Many kids like Jason feel this way. You may feel cheated. You may also feel that life is unfair. These feelings are completely normal. Don't make things worse by getting angry at yourself for feeling this way. Accept your feelings. Let people close to you know how you feel. Talking about your feelings can make you feel better.

A few months later, Jason's mother had to go back to the hospital. The cancer had come back. Jason visited her after school. He could see she was getting weaker. It was harder for her to speak.

Writing down your thoughts and emotions in a diary can often help you cope with troubling times.

Jason's aunt came to live with him and his sister. That made things at home easier.

Jason tried to cheer up his mother when he visited. But she no longer had the energy even to keep her eyes open. Jason knew she was dying. He continued to visit her. But seeing his mother so sick made Jason very upset.

Jason wanted to visit his mother. But there are many boys and girls who don't feel that way. They say that visiting their sick parents is very upsetting. These kids love their parents just as much as Jason loves his mother. But they find it very hard to visit in hospitals. There are times when a person must put aside personal feelings so they can do something more important. Sometimes it is important to grant a dying person's wish or to do things you know will make a sick person happy. Most of the time it is enough to be there and to show support. Finding the strength to put your discomfort aside is not easy. But making sacrifices for those who mean a lot to you is one responsibility of growing up.

Cancer and some other diseases can be *terminal*. This means that they cause death. When a parent has an illness that can't be cured, he or she may stay in the hospital, go home, or go to live their last days in a *hospice*. A hospice is a place for people with terminal illnesses. If your parent needs medical attention, he or she must stay in the hospital. You may want your sick parent to come home. But this is not always possible.

A terminally ill parent may be able to come home to stay with the family. Even though your parent is dying, being home can make him or her feel better. Being in familiar surroundings, close to the people he or she loves, is comforting. But you will probably have more to do around the house. You may find it difficult to act like you did before your parent got sick. This happens to many kids. Don't worry. What your parent needs most now is to be in a safe, familiar setting and to be near you, no matter how you act.

As you have already read, some people who are dying go to live at a hospice. You are allowed to visit your parent in a hospice. Doctors, nurses and counselors at a hospice are trained to work with patients who are dying. They try to make the dying person as comfortable as possible. They also work with the families. They are trained to help people deal with their feelings of grief and sadness.

No one knows, including the doctors, when a patient is going to die. Not knowing can be painful and confusing. There will be good days, when your sick parent seems to be recovering. In terminal cases the good days will not last. But your company can make the good days even better. You will be able to enjoy them with your parent.

Spending time with a terminally ill parent is difficult and scary. But when you look back on that time you will have many good memories.

Strains on the family budget may make it necessary for children to make extra money at part-time jobs.

Funerals are important rituals that allow mourners a chance to grieve and an opportunity to say a final good-bye.

Chapter 5

The Funeral

Most cultures have rituals to acknowledge death. In our culture, that ritual is called a funeral. A funeral serves many purposes. For one thing, it can help you to overcome feelings of denial. If you are still running away inside and pretending your parent is still alive, the funeral helps you to accept the truth.

A funeral can also be very comforting. It gives you a chance to mourn with family and friends who will help you to overcome your loss. Being together with other people who knew your mother or father enables you to share your sadness and remember all the good times you had with your parent.

The funeral ceremony is usually led by a religious leader such as a priest or a rabbi. This leader says prayers and words of comfort for the mourners. He or she also talks about your parent's life.

Often, friends and relatives are also given a chance to speak. They tell stories that show how much your parent was liked and respected. Someone may even tell a joke that shows your parent's sense of humor. The funeral gives people a chance to express what your parent's life and friendship meant to them.

Your living parent may decide that you shouldn't attend the funeral. She or he may think you are too young. Or he or she may think that the experience will be too painful for you. But talk it over with your parent. Explain that you understand the purpose of a funeral. Explain that you wish to say goodbye to your parent with the rest of the family and friends. Say that you will feel left out and upset if you cannot go. After you've calmly told your parent about your feelings, plan to attend.

You may decide that you don't want to attend the funeral. If you don't feel you can handle it, say no. Don't push yourself. Boys often get a hard time from the family if they say they don't want to attend. You have to make people understand how you feel.

Brian's uncle tried to bully Brian. He wanted Brian to go to his mother's funeral. "Act like a man," his uncle said. But Brian was too upset over her death. He didn't think he could handle being with so many people. He told his uncle that he loved his mother very much. But he didn't want to go.

Attending the funeral isn't a sign of how much you loved your parent. You may want to say goodbye in your own way. You may want to grieve in private. Hopefully, your family will understand if you don't want to go to the funeral.

What Happens At A Funeral

Sometimes the funeral is held in a church. Other funerals are held at places called *funeral homes.* The funeral home director and the staff will help your family with the arrangements. Some funerals are small and quiet. Some funerals are attended by a lot of people, and there are many speakers. At a church funeral, sometimes there is music by a choir, or an organist.

The wooden box that holds the body is called the *coffin.* At the funeral, the coffin may be open or closed. Some people want the coffin open. They say it is a last chance to see the dead person. Others want the coffin closed. They say they want to remember the person as he or she looked when he or she was alive.

If the coffin is open, you will have to decide whether you want to see the body. Some grown-ups may try to discourage you. Others may encourage you. There is no right decision. Whether you see the body or not won't change how much you loved your parent when he or she was alive. This isn't a test of bravery. Before you decide, think about how you will feel about seeing the body.

You may decide that you wish to speak at the funeral. This is a decision you should reach with your living parent. If he or she agrees, then you will have a chance to say a few words. You can express how much your parent meant to you. This speech is called a *eulogy*. You should write down what you want to say. You might have a short story to tell that shows your parent's understanding and love.

But don't feel that you must speak at the funeral. You may be too sad to say anything. Your family and friends understand that this is a painful and difficult time for you.

You may be surprised at the funeral by the sad reaction of other family members and friends. You may have never seen your father cry, or your mother break down. Crying is not a sign of weakness. It is a sign of grieving. Their behavior may make you uncomfortable or scared. But they are just expressing their grief. That is what a funeral is for. Don't feel that you must help your grieving parent. What you should do is deal with your own grief.

After the service at the funeral home, the body is usually taken to the cemetery for burial. Going to a cemetery is very hard. It can even be scary. But seeing the coffin put into the ground is another way to see how final the death is. And that memory will help you cope with your loss better in the time to come. Some people are placed in *mausoleums*. These are buildings where caskets are stored above ground. Spaces are cut in the walls for the coffins. These places are called vaults.

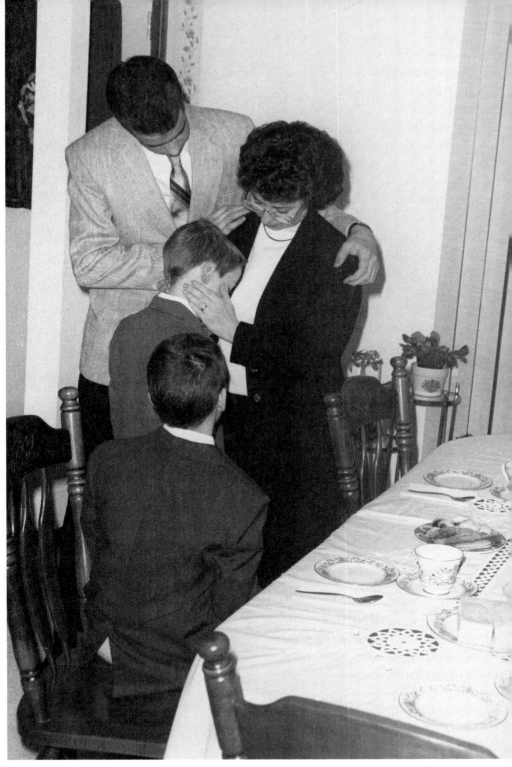

Close family and friends are an important source of support during periods of crisis.

Some people tell their families to have their body burned, or *cremated.* The remaining ashes are given to the family. Some people put the ashes in a vase called an *urn,* and keep the ashes at home. Sometimes the ashes are spread over a place that had special meaning to the dead person. Larry's father loved to fish. His ashes were scattered over his favorite lake.

Some people don't want to be buried. They write wills asking their family to give their body to medicine. Their body's organs are then used in transplants. A cornea transplant can give sight to a blind person. Some organs can be taken from a dead person to save the life of another who is sick or dying. People who donate their body to medicine say they do it because they want their last act of life to help others. But some religions forbid transplants.

There are many different ideas about what happens to people after they die. Some believe that each person has a soul that even death can't destroy. Others believe that dead people continues to live through their children. The children's lives are reflections of the lost parent. Many people feel that a dead person remains "alive" in the memories of those who knew him or her. Still other people say they don't know what happens after death. You may already have your own ideas about what happens after death. The question has no easy answers. You may find that over time you will come up with your own ideas.

Chapter 6

Moving Beyond Grief

Y our parent's death will affect you for a long time. And the process of accepting that your parent is gone is often lengthy and difficult. It is important to give yourself time to grieve. Death is a part of life, but this fact is hard for many people to face. Be patient with yourself. There is no time limit on grieving.

Learning to Accept Death

As time goes on, your parent's death will become real. You will get used to your mother or father's not being there. This is called acceptance. Acceptance is often recognized as the final stage of grieving. It doesn't mean forgetting about your parent. Acceptance simply means that you are willing to believe your parent is dead.

Even after you have accepted your parent's death, your sadness may not lessen immediately. Your emotional pain won't go away automatically because of the acceptance. It takes time to disappear. And even after you think it has gone forever, feelings such as anger, sadness, and despair can return without warning. After you have moved on with your life, you may still have bouts of intense sadness. They can be triggered by memories, photographs, experiences, or simply something someone says that reminds you of your deceased parent. These sudden feelings are normal.

When thirteen-year-old Jerome accepted that his father was dead, he stopped waiting at the front door each night for his dad to come home from work. Jerome still wishes his father were alive. But he recognizes that his father is gone and he has to continue his own life.

Acceptance also means realizing that some things are beyond our power to change. This can be a difficult lesson to learn. Almost 700 years ago, St. Francis said, "God grant me the serenity to accept the things I cannot change, the courage to change the things I can, and the wisdom to know the difference." Remembering this when you feel powerless or hopeless may help.

As you grieve, talk with someone about your feelings. A school counselor, an older relative, or a close friend can listen. Talking about your feelings helps you look at them realistically. They often don't seem so gigantic or overwhelming when you share them with someone.

After your parent dies, you may have questions about death and dying. Midori's mother died in a car accident. Midori asked her father how someone so young could die, especially when Midori needed her so much. Midori's father told her that no one knows the answer to that question. But he urged her to have faith that things would work out, and that everything happens for a

There are many ways to reach out and ask for help during times of extreme sadness. Friends, family, counselors, and hotlines are all just a phone call away.

purpose. He gave Midori the support and understanding that she needed.

Your Life Isn't Over

You also have to continue living your life, even after your parent's death. Keep yourself busy with normal activities. If you're on a team, continue playing. See friends. Go to school and club meetings. Continue to do the things you did before your parent died.

If you don't think you are ready to resume normal activities yet, try doing a project that honors the memory of your father or mother. Start writing your feelings and memories in a journal. Draw a picture or make a collage of photographs of your parent. Even the singer Madonna needed to express her feelings about the death of her mother. She wrote the song "Promise to Try" to honor her mother's memory and to give herself strength to go on with her life.

Some teenagers continue to use their parents' memories in a positive way. Carlos's father died of leukemia. Now Carlos has decided he wants to go to college to study medicine. He wants to be a research scientist and discover the cure for leukemia.

Lavetta's mother died of alcoholism. Lavetta saw the results of her mother's drinking and wanted to help others with the same problem. She decided to become a drug counselor.

When Jamal wanted to try smoking, he thought about the things his mother had taught him when she was alive. Jamal knew smoking wasn't something his

Doing things you enjoy can ease sadness after a personal tragedy.

mom would have approved of. He decided not to start.

The memories of parents can be powerful motivators. Carlos, Lavetta, and Jamal are using their parents' deaths to help them make smart and healthy choices. There are many ways to keep your parent's memory alive.

You also may want to concentrate on thinking about your future. You may still be grieving, but your parent would have wanted you to live your life to the fullest. Your parent would have wanted you to lead a happy and healthy life. Think about the wonderful things that lie ahead for you. Your parent will be with you in spirit in the years to come.

Good friends share your life with you during good times as well as bad.

Chapter 7

How to Help a Friend

Ann's Diary

Shauna is my best friend, and she came to my door in tears the day her mom died. I didn't really know how to comfort her. I had never been in that situation before, and I didn't want to say or do the wrong thing. I just gave her a big hug and invited her in. She cried on my shoulder for a while, then I cried too. Eventually we both stopped, and I asked her if she wanted to talk about it. I just tried to be as gentle and supportive as I could, and I think I helped her in some small way.

So far this book has tried to help you cope when your parent dies. But in this chapter, you will learn what you can do to help a friend who has lost a parent. He or she will need your support and love during this difficult time. In some cases, your help can save a life.

Real friends want to help. But they often feel awkward. They aren't sure what to do or say. They are afraid that they will say something stupid and make matters worse. Friends that have already lost a parent are likely to be most understanding. But even those with both parents alive can help.

As a friend, the best thing you can do is listen. Make it easy for your friend to talk about the death of a parent. Go to a place where it's quiet. Avoid noisy places, like malls and school yards. Peaceful places, such as a park or basement, are good choices.

Listening doesn't mean having the right words to say. There are no right words. It does mean letting your friend do the talking. Don't force your friend to talk about a parent's death. But tell him or her that if he or she wants to talk about it, you will listen. Not everyone grieves in the same way.

Mary Ann may need to cry. She may get angry. Don't take it personally. She has suffered a great loss. You can also expect her to say things that don't make sense. But don't correct her. She is grieving. Remember, grieving is the feeling of sadness suffered when something special is gone.

Jonathan may tell you that he feels like a stranger in his own house. There's so much activity that there is no place for him to be left alone. His parent's friends are busy making funeral arrangements and cooking food. But no one has taken a moment to talk with him. Sometimes kids get pushed aside when tragedy strikes. Adults forget that kids grieve. They think that they are too young to feel sad or to understand death. But kids get sad, too.

There are times when a friend can save a life. Watch out for danger signals. If your friend says he or she wants to join her lost parent in heaven, immediately tell her living parent. Your friend may be threatening suicide (killing herself). Don't take it as a joke. Taking it seriously could save your friend's life.

A friend may try to get you to promise not to tell anyone how he feels. But this is a promise that you should not keep. Your friend is so upset that he may feel that his own life is worthless. Your friend is wrong. At dark moments, some people are overcome by grief. They can't see the value of their own lives. As a friend, you can tell someone how much he or she means to you. But that may not be enough. Don't ignore your friend's feelings. Tell someone. The best person to tell is the living parent. If for some reason that isn't possible, tell a pastor, priest, rabbi, or school official. Don't keep it to yourself.

Your best efforts to help may not be enough. Your friend may need to get help from adults whose job it is to help people in pain. (There is a list at the back of the book that tells where people can get help. Counselors receive special training at helping others grieve. They feel comfortable talking about

death. They see it as a natural part of life. Many
hospitals and hospices employ grief counselors. A
grief counselor understands the stages of grief that
a person goes through. Pastors, priests, and rabbis
have also been trained at helping people grieve.

Remember, the best help you can give is to
make your friends understand that they are not
alone. Let them know that you care, and so do
their other friends and family. At first your friends
may not believe you. In time they will see that you
are telling the truth. With your help, and with time,
the pain will pass.

Glossary

coffin A wooden box in which a body is buried. Also called a casket.

cremate To change a body to ashes by burning. The ashes are often kept in an urn or a small jar.

defense Something you use to hold back a flood of feelings.

denial Blocking true feelings or denying reality.

depression Constant feeling of sadness.

eulogy A speech given at a funeral.

foster care Care of children by people who are not parents or relatives.

funeral A memorial service before the burial of someone who has died.

grief Intense sadness and sorrow felt after a trauma.

grief counselor A person trained to help others deal with sorrow.

hospice A place where dying people receive special care and support.

mausoleum A building where coffins are stored.

mourning The way grief is shown.

suicide The act of killing yourself.

terminal disease Illness that ends in death.

urn Container that holds the ashes of a person who has been cremated.

Where to Go for Help

Boys and Girls Clubs of America
1230 West Peachtree Street Northwest
Atlanta, GA 30309
(404) 815-5700
Web site: http://www.bgca.org

Compassionate Friends
P.O. Box 3696
Oak Brook, IL 60522-3696
(630) 990-0010
e-mail: tcf_national@ prodigy.com

**National Directory of Children's Grief
   Support Systems**
P.O. Box 86852
Portland, OR 97286
(503) 775-5683

Youth Crisis Hotline
(800) 448-4663

In Canada
YouthLink
(416) 922-3335

Internet Sites:
Grief, Loss & Recovery
http://www.erichad.com/grief

GriefNet
Sponsored by the Rivendell Foundation of Ann Arbor,
  Michigan
http://rivendell.org/

Teen Age Grief (TAG)
http://www.smartlink.net/~tag/index.html

Teen Grief Conference
Sponsored by the Bereavement Research Council
http://www.bereavement.org/teen.htm

For Further Reading

Bode, Janet. *Death Is Hard to Live With: Teenagers Talk About How They Cope with Loss.* New York: Delacorte Press, 1993.

Chelsea House Staff. *Death and Dying.* New York: Chelsea House Publishers, 1997.

Dockrey, Karen. *Will I Ever Feel Good Again? When You're Overwhelmed by Grief and Loss.* Grand Rapids, MN: Fleming M. Revell Company, 1994.

Grollman, Earl A. *Straight Talk About Death for Teenagers.* Boston: Beacon Press, 1993.

Schleifer, Jay. *Everything You Need to Know When Someone You Know Has Been Killed.* New York: Rosen Publishing Group, 1998.

Spies, Karen. *Everything You Need to Know About Grieving.* Rev. ed. New York: Rosen Publishing Group, 1997.

Index

About the Author

Fred Bratman is a freelance writer and editor whose work has appeared in leading national magazines. He has authored a book for teenagers entitled *War in the Persian Gulf*. He lives in New York City with his wife, Robin.

Acknowledgments and Photo Credits

Cover photo by Chuck Peterson; photo on p. 29 by Chris Volpe; all other photos by Stuart Rabinowitz.